PASTOR'S

WEDDING GIFT.

BY

WILLIAM M. THAYER,

AUTHOR OF "HINTS FOR THE HOUSEHOLD," "SPOTS IN OUR FEASTS OF CHARITY," ETC.

"But happy they, the happiest of their kind,
Whom gentle stars unite; and in one fate
Their hearts, their fortunes and their beings blend."
THOMSON.

"I love thee, and I feel
That in the fountain of my heart a seal
Is set, to keep its waters pure and bright
For thee." SHELLEY.

BOSTON:
NICHOLS AND NOYES,
1867.

Entered according to Act of Congress, in the year 1854, by
WILLIAM M. THAYER,
In the Clerk's Office of the District Court of the District of Massachusetts.

PREFACE.

It has become quite general for pastors to present to the couples whom they marry some token that may serve as counsellor and guide to them in their matrimonial relations. In observing this custom, the author has often realized, in the course of his ministry, the need of a larger and more comprehensive Pastor's Wedding Gift than the bookstores at present afford. For this reason he has prepared this humble volume, and now sends it forth upon its mission.

The work is written with special reference to the interest which pastors cherish in those whom they unite in marriage. It is also designed to embrace a discussion of the more important duties and principles required to make a couple happy and their home peaceful.

W. M. T.

This Certifies

That Prof. Edw. P. Evans and Mrs Elizabeth E. Gibson were united in Marriage by me, according to the Laws of the State of New York at Syracuse

May 23d 1868.

Samuel J. May.
Minister of the Gospel.

INTER. REVENUE 5 FIVE CENTS 5 INLAND EXCHANGE

CONTENTS.

PASTOR'S ADDRESS

TO

THE BRIDAL PAIR.

I.

PASTOR'S ADDRESS TO THE BRIDAL PAIR.

BRIDAL PAIR! from the circle of home, on either side, tearful eyes gaze upon your receding footsteps, and many a "God bless you!" falls from unfeigned lips. Here and there a friend, endeared by a thousand ties, would whisper in your ears some hearty counsel, and wish that it might be held as a treasure in your loving hearts. But no friend, however kind and true, will follow you with deeper interest than he, who, in the name of God, has sealed your nuptial bands. None will lift for you a heartier prayer than he. Before him the plighted vow was made, and he pronounced you "ONE." Before him, calling upon God to witness, you pledged your mutual confidence and love for life. *He* consummated the union that will add essentially to your earthly weal or woe. Untrue, indeed, would be his heart, if this solemn marriage-rite did not awaken his sincerest interest in your welfare! Unfeeling would he be, if the glad or painful tidings, borne to his ear of your course and destiny, did not excite his joy or regret!

Regard it, then, as true, wedded couple, that, while other eyes may look with indifference upon your ways, the eye of him who married you will never turn away from your life-path until it is closed in death, or you wander beyond the sphere of his knowledge and influence. The best wishes of his heart are with you, and "good news" from you and yours will be hailed with delight. What though the hand of Providence guide you to a distant clime, and he never see you more; what though other sights and scenes may blot *his* name from your memories; what though time may work its fearful changes in the circumstances and prospects of all; what though age may whiten your shining locks, and dim your laughing eyes; —*that he married you* is enough to assure his hearty response to any intelligence that may be borne to him of your hopes and destiny.

Why have you become husband and wife? Is it in obedience to an imperious demand of nature,—because the heart was made to love? Is it to lay a pure offering upon the altar of affection? I see that the human heart everywhere inclines to fasten its strong attachment upon something. From the little child in the nursery to the old man upon the borders of the grave, there is the same development. From the untamed savage in the vast wilderness to the refined and polished scholar, I see the sentiment of the poet verified:

"The heart, like the tendril, accustomed to cling,
Let it grow where it will, cannot flourish alone;
But will lean to the nearest and loveliest thing
It can twine with itself and make closely its own."

Another has beautifully said, "In the hovel among the

mountains, in the palace on the plains, in the cot by the brook, in the frescoed seat of luxury, in the abodes of the poor, and in the mansions of the rich, among the dwellers of the icy north and those of the sunny south, on the lone islands of the sea and the distant lands of blossom and song, we find the same native plant of affection growing luxuriantly; in all climes and in all places, a native everywhere, and an exotic nowhere. The Indian, in his stern, savage vigor, and wild, storm-like power, bows, a softened and subdued worshipper, at its shrine. The philosopher, in the great laboratory of nature, with her crucibles, her telescopes, her fires and her laws, scattered around him, forgets not to bring his daily gift to the shrine of the heart. The monarch of empires, the king of nations, the commander of armies, the conqueror of the world, never blots from his soul this immortal image of the God of love!"

Why, then, this plighted vow? Is it to obey the promptings of this inward sentiment, pure and lovely as can fill the soul? Then Heaven will smile upon your union, and you will bless the day that made you "ONE!" If otherwise, you have mingled for yourselves a cup of bitterness to be drunk to its very dregs. In the tones of the voice, the words of the mouth, the shades of the brow, and the sorrow of the heart, there will be a decided utterance of the ills entailed. The fountains of sympathy will be dried up, the emotions of tenderness will be eradicated, and reciprocal kindness and dewy tears will pass away. Sad blight upon the buds and blossoms of early hope and friendship!

Often ask yourselves, amid the cares and duties of life, Why this plighted vow? Perhaps it will leave a blessing behind, even though there arise no specific answer. It is well to interrogate our hearts, — well to test our sentiments and principles.

The inquiry will often arise in the heart of him who married you, Whither gone? In what neighborhood or land is their abode? What company do they gladden or annoy by their presence? As he turns over the leaves of his Pastoral Record, he reads, "On the —— day of —— married Mr. ——— and Miss ———;" and, however dim the recollection of the event because of the lapse of years, it now flashes upon his mind as if it were a fact of yesterday. Gladly would he fly on the wings of imagination to their habitation, to trace upon their brows the lines of past experience. Gone whither? he inquires again and again, nor is he satisfied with the answering echo, Whither? He would listen to some reports of their whereabouts, if not behold with his own eyes the abode where cluster their earthly hopes. He remembers a youthful couple whom he pronounced "man and wife," some years ago, on the eve of their departure to the alluring West, — and good tidings have often been borne from their home on the rolling prairie. He recalls another hopeful pair, married in his own parlor, on Christmas Eve, as fair and beautiful a bride and bridegroom as ever stood at the altar of marriage, — and they went forth to seek their fortune in the wide, wide world. The only answer ever returned to his question, Whither? has been the echo, Whither? And still another memory retains the city merchant with his blooming country bride, taken to her new and splendid home in the great metropolis. Ten years have passed away, and now he learns that fortune has smiled upon them, and they have just sailed on a pleasure-tour to the "Old World" and Palestine.

But he would learn from all whom he has introduced into this life-alliance. He would have no dark uncertainty brooding over their wanderings, no mystic veil conceal the spot where their tents are pitched. Whether reposing on a wild prairie of the West, or in the valley of its mammoth river, in rural village or crowded city, or amid strangers in distant climes,

"Over the dark blue sea,"

he would learn of their blissful or wretched homes.

Doubtless golden visions of the future are enchanting your hearts, and you scarcely indulge a doubt that your highest expectations will be realized. More is usually anticipated at the altar of marriage than is enjoyed. The matrimonial state is often hailed as an Elysian land, where sighs are all hushed, and tears are all wiped from the eyes. And it is far better that the wedded couple be full of hope and promise than saddened and dejected upon the threshold of their life-relation. Still, moderation should be exercised, lest disappointment, unexpected and severe, roll too great a burden upon their sensitive natures. There is a flattery of the future to inexperienced minds that often awakens expectations only to disappoint them. The shores of time are scattered with the wrecks of cher-

2

ished plans and hopes, destroyed by the delusive flatteries of the world.

Moderate your expectations. Be not cheated by the world's vain promises. Maintain proper and reasonable views of life. Expect little, and be prepared for much. Know that anticipation is the eclipse of realization. The honey-moon does not last forever. "It is not always May!" Winter follows the blooming beauties of summer and the "golden crops" of autumn. Clouds and sunshine alternate. Storm and calm, day and night, succeed each other. Perpetual fair weather is not well. A tempest purifies the noxious air. So human experience is checkered, changeful, sorrowful and joyous, and all the better for that. There is much truth in the following lines of Pope:

"Love, Hope and Joy, fair Pleasure's smiling train,
Hate, Fear and Grief, the family of Pain;
These, mixed with art, and to due bounds confined,
Make and maintain the balance of the mind;
The lights and shades, whose well-accorded strife
Gives all the strength and color of our life."

If you were made the recipient of all the blessings that you expect at the hand of Providence, it would doubtless prove your ruin. It would be well neither for your mind nor heart to be so blest. It is well that some of your flattering dreams are nothing more than *dreams*, — that some of the anticipated sights and scenes are mere visions of the fancy.

You go forth from a kindred circle that still has claims upon your affections. Warm hearts may yet throb therein for you. They have loved much, felt much, experienced much, for you. Possibly, some of them may have done more for your welfare than any and all other earthly friends. You, yourselves, have yet to prove that you can and will do more for each other than they have done for you. As yet you have only *promised;* it remains to fulfil. But those whom you leave behind have proved their fidelity. They have watched, toiled, wept, perhaps prayed. Their influence has been exerted,— their impression is made,— their work is done.

Forget not your father and mother, brother and sister, in your love for each other. Cherish their memories, as a precious legacy, after you bid adieu to them and the old mansion where you have safely dwelt. Often let your minds wander back to the homestead where the loved ones gathered in fond and unbroken fellowship. Forget not the shady tree and the meandering stream, on whose banks you plucked the mint and cowslip, and where you listened to the merry warblers, the robin, thrush and jay, filling the air with the music of their songs. And, O, never lose the recollection of that mother's smile, and the kind voice that enforced a father's mandate, when your childhood nestled under the wing of their affection!

These are bright mementos of the early home to be cherished when you are far away from the ancestral fireside, and will serve to connect the past and future as the uniting link of an otherwise severed chain. It is well for you to tarry at this crisis of life, and look back upon the bowers that you leave ere you too highly exalt your bridal home. It may modify your expectations, and prepare you for an ever-changeful experience. And, though the time never comes when your hopes are fully realized, giving heed to these suggestions may contribute largely to your contentment.

Still, you are to love each other more than your kindred, and your bridal more than your natal home. With the warmest, largest heart you should fill this new relation. This alone is consistent with the vow you have made, and the obligations that rest upon you. Without this there is no assurance that your home and union will be happy.

Inquiries relating to your destiny will often be made by him who married you. Does the smile of fortune rest upon them, or the blight of disappointment nip their budding hopes? Are they indulged and petted in the lap of luxury, or do they struggle and repine under the pressure of poverty? Are they successful in the pursuits of life, or do they weep over blasted expectations? Do they walk in the fear of God, or bow their hearts to Baal and Ashtaroth? Does the sweet incense of virtue, or the exhalations of vice, ascend from their path? Is religion their guide, solace and support, or are they crossing the sea of life without chart or compass? Are they serving God or the delusive world? Are they living or dead? What is their destiny?

With such inquiries the pastor will follow you from the marriage-altar into the conflicts of life. To him there is something grand in your going forth to add another to the families of earth. It is grappling with human responsibility at a crisis of life, and will plant another rose or brier in the garden of domestic experience. It is opening the door of another home whither friends will delight to wend their way. It is laying a hearthstone around which early "loves" will cluster. What affections may be nurtured there! What fountains of bliss opened! What noble purposes evolved! What anticipations realized! And, alas! (forced to view the darkest side of the picture), what feuds may be engendered! What hopes dashed! What virtues sacrificed! What hearts broken! What destruction wrought!

None more than he who married you will rejoice to hear that you are blest in basket and store. The good things of this world, in liberal measure, used as not abusing them, will contribute to your felicity; and he would have you share them by honest means and with a goodly spirit.

"A good name is rather to be chosen than great riches, and loving favor rather than silver and gold." Beautiful words of the wise man are these; and who would not delight to see them verified in your experience! It would surely gratify him who invoked the divine blessing upon your wedding-day. A name that shall be as the sweet perfume of flowers to fellow-travellers in life, may this be yours beyond the power of slander or malice to destroy! As the music of pleasant voices, and the melody of harp and timbrel, may the sound of your name fall upon every wayfarer's ear!

"A friend loveth at all times, and a brother is born for adversity." May such gather around you with the good cheer of wholesome counsel and true sympathy,— a faithful band, whose friendship is tried, and whose love faileth not! May they prove your armor-bearers and life-guards. "As the mountains are round about Jerusalem," so may their fidelity and love surround you as a bulwark of defence. And, more than all, may you enjoy the good-will of that greater, better, holier FRIEND who "sticketh closer than a brother."

Does trial come upon you when walking in the plain path of duty? The tidings awaken the sympathies of your aforenamed well-wisher. Trial in some form and measure must be experienced in this world, and, properly regarded, it comes as a "blessing in disguise." Tenderly may the blessed Lord deal with you in this regard, tempering the wind to the shorn lamb! The early rupture of your marriage-bonds by the hand of death would be deplored by him whose ministrations gave them being. Long may you walk together in the endearing relation of husband and wife, the union severed not until bowed with weary age, and parted then to renew your love amid the joys and glories of the "Better Land."

To aid you in the discharge of important duties, you will find counsels recorded in the remainder of this volume. Ponder and live them well, and great will be your reward.

"Then may the union of young hearts,
So early and so well begun,
Like sea and shore, in all their parts,
Appear as twain, but be as one.

"Be it like summer — may they find
Bliss, beauty, hope, where'er they roam;
Be it like winter, when confined, —
Peace, comfort, happiness, at home.

"Like day and night — sweet interchange
Of care, enjoyment, action, rest;
Absence nor coldness e'er estrange
Hearts by unfailing love possessed!

"Like earth's horizon — be their scene
Of life a rich and various ground;
And, whether lowering or serene,
Heaven all above it and around.

"When land and ocean, day and night,
When years and nature cease to be,
May their inheritance be light,
Their union, one eternity."

MONTGOMERY.

DUTIES

OF THE

CONJUGAL RELATION.

II.

DUTIES OF THE CONJUGAL RELATION.

You will readily admit, dear friends, the truth of the old maxim, "It is wise to weigh well what we can only once decide." A decision that is final in regard to almost any subject invests it with peculiar interest and importance. The whole responsibility with which it is fraught is crowded into that single act of the will. I remember to have seen somewhere the following incident. A ship's crew were cast upon a desolate island in a storm. The prospect of their deliverance was very dark. There was scarcely any hope of their preservation unless they could strike a fire. Preparations were made to kindle a fire, and a pile of fagots were gathered. But on opening their match-box, it contained but *a single match!* What fearful interest gathered around that single match as it was lifted to strike! Life itself was suspended upon it! If they failed in the attempt to light it, they were lost; if successful, they were probably safe.

Somewhat of that interest invests every subject when the decision that disposes of it forever is made. This is even true of those secular affairs whose importance is comparatively small. The merchant reaches a crisis in his business, when everything seems to depend upon one timely act, and the pressure of responsibility causes him to tremble as he meets it. The sailor tosses upon a stormy sea when his fate is possibly decided by the reefing of a sail or a turn of the rudder; and who can fully realize the almost crushing interest of the moment?

This truth is strikingly illustrated in the conjugal relation. Marriage is decided but once. It is a life-union. The die is cast for happiness or misery. The moment a bridal couple are pronounced "husband and wife," their destiny is fixed. What God has joined together, man cannot put asunder. Happy or not, the wedded pair must continue in the bands of wedlock. It was their own choice, — a deliberate resolve, — and they must abide the consequences. Come what may, it is done "*once for all.*" In such relations there is deep meaning in that little word, ONCE. It deserves to be pondered. It is no trifle. Nothing is trifling that confers weal or woe. "ONCE FOR ALL," — though it crushes both the wedded hearts, and a score of others with them! Once done, — done forever!

Such importance is evidently not attached to marriage by the majority of those who enter it. The relation is too often entered without considering what issues are at stake. An eminent writer says, "They who enter the marriage state cast a die of the greatest contingency, and yet of the greatest interest in the world, next to the last throw for eternity. Life or death, felicity or a lasting sorrow, are in the power of marriage. A woman, indeed, ventures most, for she hath no sanctuary to retire to from an evil husband. She must dwell upon her sorrow, which her own folly hath produced; and she is more under it, because her tormentor hath warrant of prerogative, and the woman may complain to God, as subjects do of tyrant princes, but otherwise she hath no appeal in the causes of unkindness. And, though the man can run from many hours of sadness, yet he must return to it again; and when he sits among his neighbors, he remembers the objection that lies in his bosom, and he sighs deeply."

It does not require very close observation to learn that few attach such importance to the conjugal relation. The slight regard paid to its DUTIES, on every hand, is sufficient proof of this. Every observer is forced to believe that multitudes of the married would rejoice to be released from the bonds. A writer states, as his opinion, that at least one family of every five, in the city of Boston, would be happier in being separated, than they are in dwelling together. This need not be said particularly of Boston. Something like this is true of every town and neighborhood. And it shows that there must be a great neglect of the DUTIES belonging to this relation. Such consequences are not a *necessary* result. If they were, it would be a stain upon the wisdom and goodness of Him who ordained that "they twain shall be one flesh."

To prove that I have not unduly magnified the delinquencies of married couples, let me state what I have seen with my own eyes; and probably nearly every reader will say that he has witnessed the same. Such a view of facts will prepare the way for a better understanding of the DUTIES that we may discuss.

I have seen a wife pouring her complaints into the ear

of an unmarried friend, and asserting that her early anticipations were only dreams, — that the ardent love of youth is romantic and delusive, — and that they who never marry are the more fortunate class.

I have seen a husband absent himself from his home as if it were only a place to eat and lodge, plunging into business with a sort of desperation, or seeking enjoyment among the congregated neighbors at the public inn or stores — doing this week after week, and month after month; yea, I have known him to go to the social party, or ball, leaving his invalid wife at home to entertain herself and children as best she could, — evidently depending more upon parties, clubs and balls, for entertainment, than he did upon his faithful wife and loving children.

I have seen the splendid mansion, richly furnished with all that can delight the eye or please the taste, and all done to gratify a refined and professedly pious wife; yet discontent preyed upon her heart, and her home was not such a home as she desired. If she could only be situated like Mrs. A. or Mrs. B., she should be perfectly happy, and would ask no more; but, as it is, there are too many disappointments and vexations to admit of much enjoyment.

I have seen a man control his purse with the exactness of a cashier, as he doled out "here a little and there a little" to his toiling wife, — never entrusting it to her even to carry to the store, and never giving her a fraction of a dollar to lay aside for such a use as her own wisdom and wants determine. Every cent for which she asked was parted with as if it were heartily begrudged, and his actions and looks seemed to say, "What can a woman want of money?"

I have seen another, — a husband who would think himself insulted if he were charged with unkindness, yet this charge is too tame for his cruelty. I have seen him absolutely compel his pious wife to leave her own meeting because his religious views differed from hers, thus playing the tyrant over her conscience and heart, — the worst form of tyranny with which the world is cursed, — and still having the audacity to consider himself a gentleman.

I have seen a wife so enslaved to her companion as not to dare purchase the smallest article without his consent. A book, a dress, any sort of a nicknack, offered upon the most reasonable terms by a trader at her door, — none of them can be bought until he has been consulted. He must be sent for, or the trader must call again. She may strongly desire the article, — it may even be quite necessary in the family; but it is of no use, — she is in bondage to her husband, and must wait his nod. Indeed, in works of charity, in which her brothers and sisters in Christ are engaged, she could not consult the dictates of her own conscience. Why should she? Her husband controls that. Her poor conscience cannot act except at his "say so;" she must consult *him*, and know whether she can give anything to the perishing, and, if she can, *how much*. Wonderful privilege! If this be not domestic despotism, worse than Austrian tyranny, then there is no despotism!

I have seen a husband transact his business with a studious effort to keep his wife ignorant of the true state of his affairs. All the while she supposed that he was very prosperous, and conducted her household arrangements upon a more expensive scale than she otherwise would have done. And when, at last, she received the unexpected and unwelcome tidings that her husband was a bankrupt, it well-nigh overwhelmed her. She reproached him for his secrecy, while she thought of this, that, and the other way in which she might have economized, to the no small advantage of the creditors.

I have seen a lazy husband, lounging about the streets, interested in every person's business but his own; a hanger-on at the hotel and stores, and more willing to lend a helping hand in his sick neighbor's family than in his own; while his faithful wife was toiling at home to support him and the hungry children, — up early, and late to bed, that she might have the more crumbs to drop into the open mouths of the little ones cooing in her nest, — a self-sacrificing, devoted partner, willing to wear herself out for the sake of an indolent husband and dependent babes.

I have seen a vain and wasteful wife, possessing more taste for dress than good sense, wearing property enough upon her back to clothe an ordinary family, in no sense "a keeper at home," but rather a gadding, flirting, loquacious woman, having less care of the household than the two well-paid domestics; while her indulgent husband labored hard in a somewhat prosperous pursuit to make "his ends meet," often sad and dejected because he could lay in store nothing for a "rainy day," and the infirmities of age.

I have seen the clergyman who has been asked by a

father if he would marry his daughter without making her promise to *love* her husband, inasmuch as she had no special affection for him. She was too conscientious to say, before God, that she loved him when the reverse was true; yet she could become his wife, and thus make herself and him miserable through life, with no scruples of conscience.

Who has ever seen a couple at fifty or sixty years of age apparently so well pleased with each other as they were during the first year of their married life? I do not say that such couples are not found, but are they not few and far between?

But time would fail me to enumerate all that is open to the eye of every observer, telling of the miseries that are entailed by unfortunate marriages. I have not pointed to the more revolting scenes of alienation and discord between husband and wife that are witnessed here and there; I have taken my examples from so-called respectable society, just as it appears in the most enlightened and Christian neighborhoods. The reader will readily recall scenes which have come under his observation, answering to those described above. In every one of the examples enumerated there is a violation of some conjugal duty by one or both of the parties.

And what does all this prove? Certainly, that the DUTIES of the conjugal relation receive little attention from multitudes who enter it. They seem to regard matrimony as a generous benefactress, who pours munificent gifts into the laps of all who enter her domain, without reference to fidelity on their part. Fatal delusion! The arch-fiend never invented a more successful instrument for the destruction of human happiness! The very relation, which God designed to add greatly to earthly bliss, becomes the occasion of indescribable woe.

Let us then turn to a consideration of the DUTIES involved in the marriage contract. Doubtless you desire to avoid the rocks and shoals on which other barks have split, and derive all the happiness from your new relation which it is capable of yielding. Be assured this can be done only by a faithful discharge of the DUTIES to which your attention is now earnestly invited.

The first duty that ought to be well considered is this, — to realize that true domestic happiness depends much upon the *little things* of life. Little attentions, little acts of devotion, little kindnesses, well-nigh determine the happiness of wedded life. Little neglects, little words of bitterness, little offences, mar the conjugal relation, — they are the little foxes that spoil the vines.

"A pebble in the streamlet scant
Has turned the course of many a river;
A dewdrop on the baby plant
Has warped the giant oak forever!"

Coleridge says, "The happiness of life is made up of minute fractions, the little soon-forgotten charities of a kiss, a smile, a kind look, a heartfelt compliment in the disguise of playful raillery, and the countless other infinitesimals of pleasurable thought and genial feeling." The experience of every wedded couple testifies to the truthfulness of these remarks. A few moments of reflection will satisfy the reader that such minor transactions as are scarcely thought worthy of attention essentially "make or mar" the happiness of the marriage state.

Jeremy Taylor has spoken upon this subject in such beautiful words that I quote his language at some length. "Man and wife are equally concerned to avoid all offences of each other in the beginning of their conversation; every little thing can blast an infant blossom; and the breath of the south can shake the little rings of the vine when first they begin to curl like the locks of a new-weaned boy; but when by age and consolidation they stiffen into the hardness of a stem, and have, by the warm rays of the sun, and the kisses of heaven, brought forth their clusters, they can endure the storms of the north, and the loud noises of a tempest, and yet never be broken; so are the early unions of an unfixed marriage; watchful and observant, jealous and busy, inquisitive and careful, and apt to take alarm at every unkind word. For infirmities do not manifest themselves in the first scenes, but in the succession of a long society; and it is not chance or weakness when it appears at first, but it is want of love or prudence, or it will be so expounded; and that which appears ill at first, usually affrights the inexperienced man or woman, who makes unequal conjectures, and fancies mighty sorrows, by the proportions of the new and early unkindness. It is a very great passion, or a huge folly, or a certain want of love, that cannot preserve the colors and beauties of kindness, so long as public honesty requires a man to wear their sorrows for the death of a friend. Plutarch compares a new marriage to a vessel before the hoops are on; everything dissolves its tender compaginations; but when the joints are stiffened, and are tied by a firm compliance and proportioned bending, scarcely can it be dissolved without fire, or the violence of iron. After the hearts of the man and the wife are endeared and hardened by a mutual confidence and experience, longer than artifice and pretence can last, there are a great many remembrances, and some things present, that dash all little unkindnesses in pieces."

"Let man and wife be careful to stifle little things, that, as fast as they spring, they be cut down and trod upon; for, if they be suffered to grow by numbers, they make the spirit peevish, and the society troublesome, and the affections loose and uneasy by an habitual aversation. Some men are more vexed with a fly than a wound; and when the gnats disturb our sleep, and the reason is disquieted, but not perfectly awakened, it is often seen that he is fuller of trouble than if, in the daylight of reason, he were to contest with a potent enemy."

It is the duty of husband and wife to cherish the WARMEST AFFECTION for each other. It is impossible for them to exercise that watchfulness already spoken of without this. They may highly respect each other, yet without love their union cannot be harmonious and happy. If mutual attachment does not bind them closely together, they are not disposed to overlook each other's faults, nor duly appreciate each other's excellences. Nothing can atone for the want of this charming grace. It is the harbinger of all that is good in matrimony, and the panacea for all its ills.

"Love is a star whose gentle ray
Beams constant o'er our lonely way ;
Love is a gem, whose pearly light
Oft charms us in the darkest night."

There are earthly homes in which we behold the exhibition of this virtue in all its purity. The "two hearts one," are *one* in very truth. There are no differences and altercations between them, but a sweet communion of spirit blends feeling and interest as the colors of the morning light. Nothing can exceed the beauty of such a scene, — fair type of the closer bond that will unite the saved in heaven. The discussion of the theme is marred only by the admission that such examples are exceedingly rare.

To marry for LOVE is a consideration which cannot be assailed by ridicule or argument. It is a motive that commends itself to every person's conscience as pure and lofty. On the other hand, to marry for money, or a home, or for beauty, or any other kindred object, cannot be regarded otherwise than foolish and censurable. All of these things have their place, but it is quite wide from the *first*. It may be well to possess a degree of wealth ; properly used it may become the means of extensive usefulness. But to make this the supreme object, or even to approximate to this, is certain death to domestic peace and happiness. The same may be said of beauty. We would not pronounce it worthless. It is one of the characteristics of divine works which God designed we should admire. It is a priceless boon wherever it is bestowed. Whether viewed on the wide-extended landscape, on the artist's canvas, or on the human face, it captivates the heart. From the humble violet, nestling in the waving verdure, to the majestic pine on the mountain-top, lifting high in air his crown of fairest green, beauty is a marked and bewitching quality. It has power over the human heart. And in the human form, — we cannot disguise the fact, construe it as we may, — beauty exerts a powerful influence over our natures. Still, beauty should be a minor consideration in entering the marriage state. *Alone*, it is a very trifling possession. In company with the substantial virtues it is a prize. The following sentiment of the poet contains the true idea :

"Affect not to despise beauty ; no one is freed from its dominion ;
But regard it not a pearl of price ; — it is fleeting as the bow in the clouds.
If the character within be gentle, it often hath its index in the countenance.
The soft smile of a loving face is better than splendor that fadeth quickly." *

The manner in which God addresses husbands upon this subject is very marked. It does not admit of the addition of another word to enforce this duty of love. "Husbands, love your wives, *even as Christ also loved the church and gave himself for it.* So ought men to love their wives as their own bodies." Comment can add nothing to the force of this language. Christ loved the church to that degree that he cheerfully laid down his life for it; and so ought husbands to love their wives. This is the plain import of

* Tupper.

the text. Were it fully practised what tenderness and strength of love would be witnessed! What scenes of harmony and bliss would be presented! Husbands ought to love their wives "*as their own bodies.*" If the husband "understands how he treats himself, there need nothing be added concerning his demeanor towards her; for what care does he take of his own body, and uses it with a delicate tenderness, and cares for it in all contingencies, and watches to keep it from all evils, and studies to make for it fair provisions, and is very often led by its inclinations and desires, and does never contradict its appetites, but when they are evil, and then also not without some trouble and sorrow."

Mutual respect is another duty of the conjugal relation. Every effort is put forth to gain the respect of friends and neighbors, while there is very little exertion between husbands and wives generally to win *each other's* respect. The latter is far more important of the two, and yet receives the least attention. If a man does not respect his wife he will not be likely to do much for her happiness. The same is true of the wife. Sincere affection will, indeed, do much by way of concealing faults, and thus laying the foundation for respect, but it will not do everything. A wife may render herself obnoxious to a very loving husband, and vice versa.

Do you inquire how this respect shall be nurtured? I answer, in the language of another, "If we would be respected, we should be respectable." In all circumstances of the marriage state the conduct should be controlled with reference to this object. In small as well as great things, in words as well as deeds, there must be a studied endeavor to secure this result. "There should be courtesy without ceremony; politeness without formality; attention without slavery; it should, in short, be the tenderness of love, supported by esteem, and guided by politeness."

MUTUAL COMPANIONSHIP AND SYMPATHY is another important duty. I have said before that I have seen a husband who made no more of his home than he would of a boarding-house, spending his evenings, and all other leisure hours, elsewhere, and apparently depending more upon the society of others than that of his own wife for enjoyment. The truth is very generally as follows: — for a season after marriage this duty of COMPANIONSHIP is well observed; but, by and by, the husband risks a leisure hour abroad, and then another, and another, until he is seldom found at home except for "bed and board." It is painful to see how small a proportion of husbands are really companionable at home. They may be eminently so abroad, but not in the company of their wives. If there for an evening, they make no more effort to be entertaining than an article of furniture. They have heard nor read nothing that is worthy of being rehearsed, — never have any news or plans to make known, and never know anything when asked, — and yet, away from home are delightful companions. That the hurrying, driving, exciting character of the age has somewhat to do with this is not denied. But such are the facts, account for them as we may.

In a number of the *Merchant's Magazine* is a communication, headed "Complaints of a Merchant's Wife." It may be considered the complaint of other wives also. It runs thus:

"It seems to me, at times, as if there were no more *men* left in the world; they have all become *citizens*. Their humanity seems merged in some presidency or secretaryship. They are good trustees, directors, cashiers, bankers, but they are very indifferent husbands and fathers. They are utterly without social chat; they read no pleasant books; they hate the sound of music; they visit nobody; they scarcely deign to look at the face of nature; and, for their unhappy wives, they must put up with cold looks and cold words. This is all wrong, gentlemen. It is a sad perversion of life; it is cruelly unjust to us and our daughters; and it is the too certain source of deep and lasting misery to those who indulge in it. . . . I bitterly feel and lament the want of that sympathy and communion of heart, which are so liberally promised us in the marriage-vow. Come, then, Messrs. Editors, to our relief. Here is a cause worthy of your pens. Exhort, frighten, ridicule, if you can, our erring husbands into a return to their alliance, and to a more rational and happy life."

No comments are needed upon the above. It is too true to be denied. Hence the importance of pressing this duty of *companionship* in a work like this. It is a reasonable, consistent, and very essential duty. It commends itself to the conscience and heart.

Sympathy is necessary in order to be companionable. The husband who has no sympathy in his nature ought never to have made such a vow as he did at the marriage altar. Indeed, he ought never to have become a husband. There are too many scenes and occasions in married life that demand its exercise, to excuse its absence. As much, and more, may be said of the wife. A woman without sympathy is a dishonor to her sex; she must be a rough, revolting, unseemly character..

It is often true that the trials of her situation render the wife an invalid, so that she is partially disqualified to make herself companionable. She is unable to do as wife and mother what she otherwise would. In her feebleness she certainly has more claims upon the sympathy of her husband than when in health. Yet, who has not seen men, making these very circumstances the occasion of seeking social enjoyment elsewhere, and absenting themselves from home, to the no small annoyance of their enfeebled companions? What a lack of sympathy! What a want of affection!

No wedded pair will live long together without finding abundant occasions to exercise this virtue. Both parties will experience trials enough to demand its exercise. And it is needed, too, in prosperity as really as in adversity. But in sickness, sorrow, disappointment, and every variety of trouble, it ought especially to be cherished.

> "There 's nought in this bad world like sympathy;
> 'T is so becoming to the soul and face.—
> Sets to soft music the harmonious sigh,
> And robes sweet friendship in a Brussel's lace." *

* Byron.

It is the duty of husband and wife to *overlook each other's faults.* Of course there is a limit to such counsel as this, but its application will be readily appreciated. However good the married parties may be, neither of them are perfect. Both have faults, and time will surely reveal them. If there be not a disposition to overlook and forgive these errors, they will become, at once, a bone of contention. It is here that multitudes in the marriage state fail, and part with connubial happiness. There seems to be a disposition in the human heart to put the worst construction upon a partner's faults; while the opposite ought to be the case. It is the dictate of reason and conscience that the most favorable view of such errors should be instituted. This spirit alone is really humane and Christian. And how beautiful the exhibition! In perfect harmony with the nature of the conjugal relation!

"Forgive and forget! — why, the world would be lonely,
The garden a wilderness left to deform,
If the flowers but remembered the chilling winds only,
And the fields gave no verdure for fear of the storm." *

MUTUAL COÖPERATION in all the toils and responsibilities of the marriage state is still another duty. It is true, husband and wife have each a separate sphere in which to act, and it is necessary that they keep within them. Still, this can be done, while they are careful to render that mutual assistance which affection and duty demand. There are many ways in which a faithful husband can

* Swain.

assist his wife in her domestic duties; and so a wife may render herself equally helpful to her husband in his secular pursuit.

Upon this subject Dr. Humphrey says, "We see that, wherever they are united as husbands and wives, different classes of duties may devolve upon them. God has made them so Their physical constitutions are in some respects so different, that, to secure connubial harmony, the man must keep within his own allotted sphere, and the woman within hers, as each of the planets must move in its own orbit, to preserve the balance of the solar system. The only way to keep the balance and maintain perfect harmony between them is for Jupiter and Venus to roll on in their respective celestial pathways." The truth is here strongly presented, yet it is not at all incompatible with mutual assistance. Coöperation does not necessarily involve a meddling, dictatorial spirit. Properly regarded, it implies the reverse.

As the result of such coöperation there will be MUTUAL CONSULTATION, — a duty which is too generally neglected. It seems to be usually conceded by the married parties that the wife shall control the household affairs, and the husband his secular business, without conferring with each other. Men are disposed to think that their wives know little about business, and hence it is quite useless to confer with them. On the other hand, women are convinced that men are so ignorant of what appertains to their domestic duties, that it would be a waste of breath to seek their advice. Hence, examples of mutual consultation in matrimony are exceedingly rare. But, in opposition to all such views and feelings, we do not hesitate to affirm that, generally, husbands would be more successful in their business relations if they consulted their wives, and wives would more prosperously conduct their household affairs if they conferred with their husbands. Their union would certainly appear more harmonious and happy.

There are other duties involved in the conjugal relation which we have not time nor space to discuss. A few of them are inseparably connected with those enumerated, and will be readily understood. Some of them may be suggested at this point, and then dismissed. AMIABILITY or GOOD TEMPER, INDUSTRY, ECONOMY, CONFIDENCE and MEEKNESS, are all indispensable to a happy union. Their absence will leave the relation open to the inroads of a fault-finding and unamiable spirit. They will, however, quite naturally succeed the cultivation of those virtues already presented.

The subject ought not to be dismissed without reference to another and more important topic, although it will receive attention in a subsequent part of the work. *The duties of the conjugal relation cannot be fully discharged without the aids of Christianity.* The parties must be CHRISTIANS in order to possess such a spirit as will ensure peace and joy until they are separated by death. If there be a wedded couple who are as happy in each other's society thirty years after their marriage as they were during the first month of their union, that couple will be found to be Christians. Love that is tried by the vicissitudes of successive years, and all the while maintains its strength and purity, if it does not actually increase in a good degree, is such as the Gospel of Christ regulates and fosters by its regenerating and conservative influence. To any bridal pair, who are desirous of perpetuating their affection warm and vigorous as it is now in the morning of wedded life, I would say, *be devoted Christians.* If now you are strangers to a saving interest in Christ, make it your first business to become the true children of God, as the most successful way to nurture and strengthen your present attachment. Religion contains not only the germ of virtues that will shine forever in the Paradise above, but of all those lesser graces that adorn life within the domestic circle. Says John Angell James, "A good Christian cannot be a bad husband and father; and, other things being equal, he who has most piety will shine most in all the relations of life. A Bible placed between man and wife as the basis of their union, the rule of their conduct, and the model of their spirit, will make up many a difference, comfort them under many a cross, guide them in many a strait wherein flesh and blood will be confounded and at a loss, support them in their last sad parting from each other, and reünite them in the world where they shall go no more out."

Perhaps you, dear friends, are both the disciples of Christ. If so, be careful that you assist each other in your Christian course. In no particular can you be more truly helpmates than in this regard. In none is it more important to be mutually faithful. In none is it easier to be negligent and inconsistent. Beware that you do not hinder each other in the way of life. Let that beautiful scene appear in your earthly union, — two followers of Christ, united by the strongest ties of love, studying to advance each other in holiness, that, at last, after the parting of earth, they may participate together in the closer communion of heaven.

Perhaps one of you is unconverted, and the other a member of the church. Without discoursing upon the right or wrong of such a union, a word of counsel will not be amiss. Admitting such a union to be wrong, it is now too late to retrieve the error. With yourselves the step is taken, and what is done cannot be undone. You must now make the best of it. Evil does not *necessarily* result from such a union. The pious party does not become worldly, and reproach religion in the eyes of his or her companion, because there is no escape from this melancholy result. Many instances might be cited to show that Christian fidelity has resulted in the salvation of the unconverted party. All such examples ought to lead the Christian husband or wife to be very faithful to the soul of his or her companion.

It is not often true that pious men marry unconverted females; but the instances are very numerous where Christian females take worldly men for their husbands. The Scriptures appear to recognize this fact, and tender important counsels to wives in such circumstances. They are exhorted to be exemplary disciples in all their conduct before their husbands, "that they may be won by the conversation of their wives, while they behold your chaste conversation coupled with fear." Religion must be happily illustrated in their lives if they would win their partners to Christ; for almost their only hope, apart from the direct agency of God, lies here, — in the beauty and power of a consistent and holy example. And, again, here is a very touching appeal: "What knowest thou, O wife, whether thou shalt save thy husband?" Perhaps your fidelity will bring him to the cross. What a powerful motive this! To be instrumental in saving a husband, what sacrifice would a Christian wife not make for this! Ponder it, thou hopeful bride, and let the thought beget the noblest aims! In the language of Mr. Jay, "Think of happiness, — the honor that awaits you. What is the triumph you have acquired over him by your charms compared with the victory you will obtain over him by your religion? What pleasure will attend you the remainder of your days! Now you are 'one heart and one mind;' now you 'take sweet counsel together.' And what will be your joy and crown of rejoicing in that day, when, before assembled men and angels, he will say, O, blessed be the Providence which attached us in yonder world, and has still more perfectly united us in this! The woman thou gavest to be with me led me not to the tree of knowledge of good and evil, but to the tree of knowledge which is in the midst of the Paradise of God."

We have now considered the leading DUTIES involved in the conjugal relation. In a matrimonial character, formed after the model described, the several virtues appear as "apples of gold in pictures of silver." A single defect will destroy the fair proportion and beautiful symmetry of the whole. Here, as elsewhere, "there is a place for everything, and everything in its place." Love, confidence, forbearance, attention, and kindred graces, must stand in their respective relations, or some unhappiness will result to the wedded pair.

The same is true of everything. Beauty itself loses half its charms unless it appears in company with other attractions. The richest, most finished painting is complete in all its parts. Not only the tree, hill and shrubbery, must be beautiful in themselves, but the *background* must be executed with equal skill. Light and shade must mingle there in richest blendings, or the whole painting is marred. It is beauty set in deformity. Thus nicely-wrought specimens of art may lose a portion of their attractions by appearing in company with defects.

So with character. A real excellence may be grouped with such deformities as to lose its lustre in part. Beauty, gracefulness, and intelligence, are a lovelier trio than beauty, awkwardness, and ignorance. So love, confidence, and forbearance, are more winning in the marriage state than love, confidence, and fretfulness. Love, in company with the former virtues, is "an apple of gold in pictures of silver."

For this charming sympathy of character in the matrimonial state may you strive. Your efforts to this end will scatter blessings all along your future pathway. Amid the trials and sad hours of life, such a character will cheer as the bright bow upon the bosom of a cloud. And, at the end of life's journey, delightful memories will throng your minds, and celestial consolations fill your hearts.

4

"From that day forth in peace and joyous bliss,
They lived together long without debate;
Nor private jars, nor spite of enemies,
Could shake the safe assurance of their state."

SPENSER.

DEDICATION

OF THE

BRIDAL HOME.

III.

DEDICATION OF THE BRIDAL HOME.

Home! No word awakens so many associations as this, and none appeals more powerfully to the human heart in all climes and circumstances. In every age and nation mankind have expressed similar sentiments, and indulged kindred feelings in relation to it. However stinted in the measure of earthly goods, it has ever possessed attractions more powerful than those of lordly "pleasures and palaces." A glad response has been awakened in every heart to the beautiful sentiment of the poet:

> "'Mid pleasures and palaces though we may roam,
> Be it ever so humble, there's no place like home." *

It has a strong hold upon the heart of the aged wayfarer and prattling child. The joyous youth hails it with his heart's warmest attachment. The weary traveller anticipates its clustering joys, as often as his thoughts turn to it in a far-off land. The exile consumes many tardy hours in cherishing its pleasant memories. The sailor forgets it not upon the raging sea. The soldier remem-

* Payne.

bers it fondly on the tented field. In short, none are so isolated in their feelings, or so abandoned to vice, as not to experience, at times, the power of HOME over their natures.

A distinguished writer says, "Home is a genuine Saxon word; a word kindred to Saxon speech, but with an import common to the race of man. Perhaps there is no other word in language that clusters within it so many and so stirring meanings, that calls into play, and powerfully excites, so many feelings, so many faculties of our being. 'Home,' — say but the word, and the child that was your merry guest begins to weep. 'Home,' — play but its tunes, and the bearded soldier, that blenched not in the breach, droops and sickens, and dies. 'Home,' — murmur but its name, and memories start around it that put fire into the brain, and affections that almost suffocate and break the heart, and pictures that bewilder fancy with scenes in which joy and sorrow wrestle with delicious strife for possession of the spirit. 'Home,' — what does it not stand for, of strongest, most moving associations! — for childhood's grief and gladness; for youth's sports, and hopes, and sufferings, and passions, and sins; for all that brightened or dimmed the eyes; for all that convulsed or tranquillized the breast; for a father's embrace, or for his death-bed; for a mother's kiss, or for her grave; for a sister's love, or a brother's friendship; for hours wasted, or hours blest; for peace in the light of life, or fears in the shadows of perdition. Home, when it is all that nature and grace can make it, has a blessedness and beauty of reality that imagination, in its fairest pictures, would find nothing to excel."

The same writer drops such honeyed words that I quote again. "The sentenced culprit, during even his last night on earth, must sleep, and perchance may dream, and seldom will that dream be all in the present and in prison; not all of it, if any, will be of chains and blood, of shapeless terrors, and pale-faced avengers, of the scaffold and the shroud. Far other things will be in the dream. He once was honest, and spent his childhood, it may be, in a rustic home, and grew to youth amidst laborious men, and with simple nature. Out of imagery thus derived will his dream be formed. In such dreams will be the green fields and wooded lane; the boat sleeping on the stream; the rock mirrored in the lake; the shadow watched expectingly from the school-room window, as it shortens to the noon-tide hour. Then there will be parents blessed in their unbroken circle; there will be young companions, laughing in their play; there will be family-greetings, thanksgiving feasts; there will be the grasp of friendship; there will be the kiss of love. The dream will not be entirely, if at all, a dream of crime, disgrace and death; it will be one that reproduces, on the brink of eternity, the freshness of emotion, hope, and desire, with which existence on earth began."

Remember, then, WEDDED PAIR, that you are to make a HOME, — a sweet bower of peace and joy in this desert world, where hope brightens, and love gathers its linked, confiding circle; — a blissful retreat for jaded and weary hearts when the busy world drives on its votaries in the train of Mammon and pampered self; — a safe and alluring shelter for *yourselves* amid the vicissitudes of life, becoming more and more the abode of peace and love as the world grows dark without, and never more blessed and precious than when about to be exchanged for a brighter home hereafter.

You are to make a HOME! Beware lest the beginning of the enterprise germinate the seeds of discord. Let it be dedicated to truth, virtue, religion, and to God. Let the first sun that rises upon it behold whatsoever is lovely and of good report. As is the beginning so will be the end. The very first day, or week, that you spend in your new residence may determine its future character. Begin well here, and you will doubtless end well. On the other hand, spurn all good advice, and enter your new home regardless of your moral obligations, and of those truths and duties indispensable to a happy family, and you may confidently expect to reap a harvest of bitterness and sorrow. Here have been sowed the seeds of almost every matrimonial rupture that has occurred. A false idea, a wrong principle, an evil, and even a reckless determination, about duty and responsibility at this period of life, has been followed, often, with a train of miseries too revolting to be described.

It is painful to behold the number of earthly homes from which the last traces of virtue and happiness have departed. In the very morning of their existence, how many become the abodes of harpy passions and godless demeanor! As if there were no God to serve, and no salvation to work out, how utterly devoid are many of everything that savors of religion! How many begin and end their existence with no reference to human accountability, and the future world!

I repeat, DEDICATE YOUR BRIDAL HOME TO GOD. It *will have* a character whether you choose or not. Give it the impress of religion, that its character may be pure, and then all the influences which it puts in circulation will be salutary.

Many seem strangely to infer that religion and domestic felicity are incompatible with each other, — that the home of the Christian graces is devoid of that cheerfulness and pleasure, without which, life moves on amid darkling shadows. Nothing can be more distant from the truth. A single incident in the life of our Saviour is replete with instruction upon this subject. It is a fact which has probably been read and discussed more than almost any scene in his eventful history.

It was the wedding-scene in Cana of Galilee. Christ was an invited guest; and his presence alone, with what he said and did, has given a distinction to that marriage beyond the nuptials of the proudest kings and queens. True, this marriage has a place on the sacred page in order to record the beginning of the Saviour's miracles. But then, if Christ began his miracles at a wedding, what lesson may we derive from the fact? Surely this, — that the gospel is friendly to matrimonial alliances, and exerts its power to render them happy.

There was evidently design in beginning his miracles at a marriage. It was not mere accident. He might have commenced them elsewhere; and it were easy to suggest some reasons for beginning them at another time. But he had a mission to perform at that time and place. So he went to the wedding, — a cheerful guest, — and there he converted water into wine. He thus contributed to the conviviality and enjoyment of the occasion. The act proved that Christ was interested in human joys, and that his religion was not a foe to smiles and innocent delights. It was not absolutely necessary that the water should be converted into wine; the couple might have been married without such a miracle, and the numerous guests might have rejoiced as sincerely with the wedded pair. But, regarding the customs of that age, we are forced to conclude that the wonderful act contributed to the enjoyment of the occasion.

Is religion, then, a foe to connubial happiness? Behold Christ rejoicing at a nuptial ceremony with those who rejoice; as at the grave of Lazarus he wept with those who wept; as if to declare that his feeling heart could respond to emotions of joy, as well as to those of sorrow; that, while he came to sympathize with, and save man, a fallen, ruined, ungrateful sinner, he recognized him to be a social being, the necessary possessor of hopes and joys, fragile as "things of air," yet all the more precious for that! Yes, Christ did not always look upon the dark side of humanity and this fleeting world when he sojourned in the flesh. He saw too much in the varied relations of life that is precious, and which his holy religion might purify and transform into celestial worth and beauty, to turn away from the view of human joys. And, were he here in person to-day, he would rejoice with you in this life-alliance, and tell you how to live to render your home happy. Yea, he would cheerfully enter into the minutiæ of life's duties, and tell you what words to utter, what precepts to cherish, what principles to maintain, how you ought to treat each other, and how you should treat your friends; in short, he would exhibit the deepest interest in all that pertains to domestic happiness. And more, he would show, what has always been illustrated in the progress of his religion, that it not only befriends the ties and enjoyments of married life, but purifies and hallows them beyond all the devices and arts of human wisdom and affection.

If such a view of Christ and his gospel were universally enjoyed it would produce a wonderful change at marriage altars and in bridal homes! That popular infidelity which lingers around the threshold of domestic life would be dissipated, and all the false views and sentiments, relating to personal piety at the fireside, would be exploded. Now, judging from observation, the belief is quite common that the presence of Christ at a wedding-scene would spoil the pleasure of the occasion. If he were now sojourning with us, he would be the very last invited guest in a majority of instances; and the knowledge of his expected presence would deter multitudes from participating in the nuptial festivities. He would be the last visitor whom many a bridal pair would desire to receive. They would expect to bid adieu to cheerfulness, ease and comfort. Yet, the wedding party at Cana were more indebted to Christ for the enjoyment of the occasion than to any other guest. The reader cannot fail to perceive this point of vital interest.

Away, then, wedded pair, with all such false conceptions of the gospel of Christ! Ponder the scene that we have feebly portrayed until you are satisfied to welcome Christ to your new residence as a Friend. Banish every feeling and sentiment that does not honor religion, and, on the first day that you tarry in the bridal home, dedicate it to the Lord.

Among the religious provisions you make for your home give the SABBATH a place. It is truly the "pearl of days." Properly observed, its benign influence will fall upon all other days of the week with a blessing. There is no fact in providence more clearly observable than this, — the blessing of God has rested upon those who have *remembered the Sabbath day to keep it holy.* Even if there were no hereafter for which to prepare, no account to render at the bar of God, it comes ladened with temporal good to every person. Deprived of its weekly visits you would part with a multitude of mercies for which you now give the day no credit. Your home would be less a home, and your marriage less a marriage.

Many pastors observe to their grief that often those who were constant in their attendance upon the means of grace on the Sabbath, before their marriage, afterwards are frequently missed from the congregation. For some reason public worship seems to have less hold upon them. They appear to attach less importance to the institution. Whatever may be the reason of this change, it is certainly a great delinquency. If two persons ever need a Sabbath for its hallowing and sanctifying influence, it is when they dedicate their bridal home, and thus prepare the way for a rising family. If they discard it, then nothing less than the sovereign grace of God will ever lead them to ask for its return.

Decide in the commencement, — WE WILL HAVE A SABBATH. Let it be a settled principle with you to visit the sanctuary both parts of the day unless Divine Providence hinders. Never allow a trivial excuse to detain you. Endeavor to realize that the habit has much to do with the character of your home, as well as with your own characters. Yes, it certainly will leave its impress upon your own characters. You will be mutually better and happier for it. Friends will love you more, and the favor of God will rest upon you.

To test your own feelings upon this subject permit me to present before you two couples, married about the same time, and in similar circumstances in regard to worldly possessions. The first entered upon the duties of domestic life with as much reason to recognize God as any other wedded pair. Yet God was not in all their thoughts. The Sabbath was to them, indeed, a rest from toil, but it was devoted to pleasure. They did not go to the house of God, nor look with approbation upon religious enterprises. Light, pernicious reading, magazines, newspapers, and novels, occupied much of their time on this holy day. Visitors were frequently received, and visits as frequently made. Rides and walks for pleasure were unscrupulously enjoyed. And thus the Sabbath was not only desecrated, but absolutely made a day of more frivolity and sin than any other day of the week. Nor is this an isolated case. There are multitudes of just such examples even in the most enlightened and Christian communities.

The other couple (I remember them well, — strongly attached to each other, and recognizing their accountability to God) dedicated their new home to Christ. The Sabbath was to them a day of religious services. Nothing but the absolute intervention of Providence detained them from the sanctuary. They were always seen in their seats, and their very demeanor was evidence of their thoughtfulness and reverence for God. At home, the day was sacredly kept. The Scriptures and religious books were the only volumes perused; and, as they never thought of visiting upon this day, so others never proposed to visit them; and as for rides and walks for pleasure, the thought of engaging in them was never indulged for a moment. I need not add that they were highly respected, and that their influence was of the most marked and salutary character.

The two pictures are before you. They speak for themselves. Which is the more worthy of imitation, which is the more lovely and beautiful, which is the more compatible with the relations of immortal and accountable beings, your better judgment will readily decide.

Then, make the latter portrait your pattern and guide in regard to the observance of the Sabbath. All your interests connubial, social, moral, temporal and eternal, demand it. It will be better for you and your friends, better for society and the world; for it will contribute essentially to the general cause of virtue. And it becomes accountable beings to remember that

> "The only amaranthine flower on earth
> Is virtue ; the only lasting treasure, truth." *

Your home will not be thoroughly furnished without the BIBLE occupies a prominent place. It is impossible to find a prosperous and happy home where the Bible is not. Observation in any community will reveal the fact that families are blest just in proportion to their regard for the word of God. Even where it is nominally received and exalted, but lies "a dead letter" upon the shelf, there is found little or none of that moral thrift and beauty which a sincere study of its truths is sure to beget.

The Bible, then, has a prominent claim upon your regard as a book of frequent reference and study. You will need, at all times, its wholesome moral and religious counsels. You will never find yourselves in circumstances where you can safely abandon its guiding light. In prosperity it will prove a prudent and wise *Telemachus*, reminding you of the goodness of him who blesses you with his bounties, and checking those desires and emotions that are prone to run wild amid the smiles of worldly fortune.

You would highly value a book that might contain important hints and lessons relating to your daily pursuit. Men have their guides in the various trades and mechanic arts, as well as in the matter of domestic economy. Scarcely a wife thinks of pursuing her housekeeping

* Cowper.

duties without a manual to instruct her in the culinary art. But the moral and religious duties which you owe to each other, and those around you, are infinitely more important than all that pertains to mere secular and domestic arrangements. And here the Bible is presented as a manual in the moral department of your home. No other book is like it. Among the countless number of volumes that are thrown off from an over-burdened press. from year to year, it has no competitor. It contains lessons of wisdom for every relation of the family, and for every circumstance and condition of married life. It has lessons for the husband and wife, for parent and child. No duty will arise in your matrimonial connection upon which it will not shed light. You can imagine no perplexing or afflictive scenes for which it is not competent to instruct or console. And, with it in your hands, you can never be excused for a breach of your plighted vow on the ground that instruction is wanting.

And, yet more, unless Providence metes out an unusual experience to you, the season of trial and sorrow will come. Somewhere in the future there is doubtless a sad hour, and a bitter cup for you. Earthly ties are very dear, and as frail as they are dear; and where they are not sundered, their very existence is often necessarily attended with great trials. For such an hour the Bible is an indispensable counsellor. Its words of encouragement and solace are full and ample. In the death-hour, especially, when the nuptial bonds, so dear beyond the power of language to describe, are about to be broken, its precious hopes and promises your sinking natures will require. O, cherish it for that season, and your last hours will be joyous and seraphic as those of sainted worthies already passed to their reward! Baxter exclaimed, in his expiring moments, "I am almost well!" Owen raised his hand, and said to a friend, "O, brother, the long-looked-for day is come at last, in which I shall see the glory of Christ in another manner than I have ever yet done!" Evarts shouted, "Glory! Jesus reigns!" and closed his eyes in death. Payson exclaimed, in his conflict with the last enemy, "The battle is fought! the battle is fought! and the victory is won forever!" Indeed, I have just returned from the death-bed of a young and excellent wife and mother, who said, as she lifted her eyes to greet me, "I am almost home! I am almost home!"

Cherish the Bible as fondly as did these departed saints, and your home will be bright and joyous in the darkest hour of sorrow, and your last end will be peace.

"Star of Eternity! the only star
By which the bark of man could navigate
The sea of life, and gain the shores of bliss
Securely! only star which rose on time,
And on its dark and troubled billows, still
As generation, drifting swiftly by,
Succeeded generation, threw a ray
Of heaven's own light, and to the hills of God,
The eternal hills, pointed the sinner's eye." *

In dedicating your bridal home to God, PRAYER is indispensable. Morning and evening, at least, the incense of

* Pollok.

grateful and loving hearts ought to ascend to God. It is not only a great privilege, but it is more, — an imperative DUTY. God expects to be thus recognized as the "giver of every good and perfect gift." Your relations, as dependent beings, render the act peculiarly appropriate. To live as a large majority of wedded couples do, with scarcely any recognition of an overruling Providence, is inconsistent with all our natural relations.

That prayer is attended with marked benefits to the family, must be admitted without accumulated proof. From its nature alone we should infer that it must have a salutary influence upon all who engage in the exercise. The husband, who sincerely brings his family to the throne of grace in observance of this rite, must be a better husband; and his wife, sincerely uniting with him, must be a better wife. If they have children and domestics, the influence upon them must be very marked and beneficial. It must allay the heat of passion, soften the asperities of temper, and regulate those desires, which, unrestrained, introduce discord and misery into the household. It must sweeten the disposition, cultivate amiability, and beget a forgiving spirit, all of which is indispensable to a peaceful home.

Dr. Alexander says, of this family rite, "Nothing tends so directly to break a channel for right influences, as the regular and faithful observance of domestic worship. A word fitly spoken, at such a time, is an apple of gold. A psalm, rightly chosen, and sung with the spirit and understanding, may bear up all hearts to God. A prayer, 'in the Holy Ghost,' though issuing from one who has not the lips of the eloquent, may go more deeply into the soul of the prodigal son, or the careless neighbor, than all the sermons of the year. These are influences which are undervalued, because they are not singly powerful, yet when constant they are mighty; they drop as the rain, and distil as the dew, 'as the small rain upon the tender herb, and as the showers upon the grass.' In the day of judgment and revelation, it will perhaps appear, in the case of many, that they have owed more in regard of individual piety to the operation of family religion, than to any single class of causes."

Above all the considerations presented is another more important. Prayer has power with God. His answering mercies descend upon the faithful suppliant, and upon those who are the subjects of his petitions. It is also a relief and source of comfort amid the cares, doubts, anxieties, pains and sorrows of life.

"Prayer is the golden key that can open the wicket of Mercy;
Prayer is the slender nerve that moveth the muscles of Omnipotence.
Wherefore, pray, O creature, for many and great are thy wants:
Thy mind, thy conscience, and thy being, thy rights commend thee unto prayer,
The cure of all cures, the grand panacea of all pains,
Doubt's destroyer, ruin's remedy, the antidote to all anxieties!" *

Perhaps, in answer to all that has been urged upon your attention, you will say, "We are not religious; we do not profess to be Christians." And what if you are

* Tupper.

not the professed followers of Christ? The truths presented have a claim upon all mankind. It is the duty of all, saints or sinners, to keep the Sabbath, cherish the Bible, and maintain daily prayer. If any persons are not prepared for these duties, by a consecration of themselves to God, it is their duty to yield their hearts at once to Christ, that they may be prepared to meet these obligations. You may not be the avowed friends of Christ, but ought you not to be? You may not have a heart to pray, but ought you not to have such a heart? Then the path of duty is plain; and that is the only path of wisdom and peace.

But, though you are not Christians, you doubtless desire to be moral, and lend your example and influence to the common cause of virtue. Even this cannot be done without a Sabbath and Bible. Trample upon the former, and reject the latter, and you cannot be even moral. So that, after making all due allowance for speaking to you in the foregoing as if you were the children of God, the sentiments advanced are still, in the main, applicable to yourselves. You have a home, and you are obligated to make it a happy home if possible. Hence, if the duties discussed, relating to the Sabbath, Bible and prayer, are essential to this end, I see not how you can elude the drift of all that has been said.

If you practise upon the foregoing counsels, and thus impart a religious character to your home, it will become to you and yours as a "green sheltered islet amid the great waves of an unquiet world." Wherever religion is allowed to diffuse itself, it purifies, and causes beauty and loveliness to put forth as the first flowers of spring. It does not nip the sweet amiabilities and graces of loving natures, as the early frost nips the blossoms of September, but gradually unfolds their charms to the view of increasing admirers. What is beautiful in the human heart religion makes more beautiful; what is innocent and delightful it embalms, after adding essentially to its attractions. Thus it may be with your bridal home. Allow the presence of this celestial messenger to hallow it, and you will never regret the act to the day of your death.

To both of you, home should ever be the centre of attraction; and a due regard to the truths and principles discussed will surely make it so. Your aims, plans and deeds, ought to point to this desirable object. It is the sphere in which God evidently designs that you should render yourselves useful, and contribute to the general good of society. I doubt if you, or any other persons, can do so much for society by the more noisy and public agencies of good, as you can in the family circle. Every model home leaves its mark upon the world. All the influences emanating from it are of the most exalted and salutary character. It sends forth good citizens to sustain order and virtue. It is friendly to good government and good institutions. It contributes to the strength and perpetuity of church and state. Hence, the most successful way for you to increase your usefulness may be to make home the great centre of attraction. Though duty and business may necessarily demand the frequent absence of the husband from it, yet, all the aims and enterprises of life centring here, it will never lose its high place in the affections. Live for home. Labor for home. Plan for home. Next to supreme love to God, let its claims lie upon your hearts.

Here it should be remarked that the peculiarities of the present age are inimical to a model home. There is much in society to wean the *husband*, especially, from this little realm. There is excitement and hurry in almost every pursuit. As another has said, "The former systems of regularity and stability are broken up, and the people not only travel by steam, and send their thoughts to their distant friends on the wings of the lightning, but the whole routine of life is performed in the same hurried manner. The notions and habits of the past generation are too staid and too slow to suit the fiery spirit of the present day. Men are not contented to grow rich, to grow in wisdom, and scarcely in stature, but they must jump from poverty into princely wealth, from a state of ignorance into men of great learning, and from a child in leading-strings into a full-grown man." In such a state of things home is likely to be more or less neglected, and much of its wholesome and needful power is lost.

Also, there is connected with this state of things another development, viz., married couples appear to be toiling, not for a present, but a future, *ideal* home. Multitudes are not at all satisfied with present materials for making a happy home, and, indeed, many seem to enter the marriage state under the conviction that their home will not, and cannot be, what they desire until certain anticipated objects are secured. The home which they possess at the commencement of wedded life is not such an one as satisfies their desires; and they have no intention of being satisfied with it. More property, ampler accommodations, additional style and luxury, these and kindred things are expected before they can really set about making a model home. Scarcely any views can be more destructive to matrimonial happiness than these. If a couple cannot be satisfied with their home at the beginning of married life, they probably never will be. Something is wrong. They do not love home for the sake of those who dwell therein, and this is enough to embitter the whole of life.

Let me reiterate, bridal pair, these needful counsels. Welcome Christ to your home. Let the gospel hallow it. Make it the centre of hope and joy. Live for it. Be content with the home that you now have, and not wait for one you may never possess. A hovel may be a happy home to those who truly love each other.

There is a brighter HOME than that of earth. Eye hath not seen, nor the heart of man conceived, the glories which fill that blest abode. It is the resort of happy, holy spirits. It is loved for its own sake. No ransomed soul anticipates a fairer mansion. There is no sickness there. Sorrow and weeping never invade the peaceful circle. Its joys never cease. Its hopes never die. The union is eternal.

MAY YOUR EARTHLY BE EXCHANGED AT DEATH FOR A HEAVENLY HOME!

"O, talk to me of heaven! I love
To hear about my home above;
For there doth many a loved one dwell
In light and joy ineffable.

O, tell me how they shine and sing,
While every harp rings echoing,
And every glad and tearless eye
Beams like the bright sun gloriously!
Tell me of that victorious palm
   Each hand in glory beareth;
Tell me of that celestial calm
   Each face in glory weareth!"

LAST WORDS

WITH

THE BRIDAL PAIR.

IV.

LAST WORDS WITH THE BRIDAL PAIR.

Before we close this interview, dear friends, let us gather up the thoughts that cluster about the conclusion of such an important subject. You must be persuaded, from the foregoing, that you have entered into no trifling alliance. You must feel that the most important act of your lives is this which has united your destinies. And, also, you can but know that your heart-hopes will be realized or dashed, according as you discharge mutual duties. Now, these hopes are many and bright, and no merciless decree of Jehovah dooms them to disappointment. If they perish with the flight of years, it will be solely on account of failure on your part. Some want of fidelity will be the cause of the sad result.

Hope is now the very life and soul of your felicity. It is delightful to hope, and we are daily "hoping on, hoping ever."

> "Hidden, and deep, and never dry,
> Or flowing or at rest,
> A living spring of hope doth lie
> In every human breast." *

* Mrs. Wells.

But you must feel, after all that has been said, that heart-hopes need to be tenderly cherished. They should be dealt with as angel-visitants, carefully entreating them, lest they be put to flight. Hopes dashed are as fruitful of anguish as hopes realized are full of bliss. All great blessings leave a deep void and bitter regrets when they are sacrificed. Learn a valuable lesson from this.

Goldsmith penned the following beautiful lines:

"Aromatic plants bestow
No spicy fragrance while they grow;
But, crushed or trodden to the ground,
Diffuse their balmy sweets around."

Thus let it prove with your earthly hopes. May they be so cherished and regarded as to "diffuse their balmy sweets" even when "crushed" by disappointment.

In the foregoing we have employed some familiar terms that possess peculiar significance, and their meaning is not fully appreciated. They have a claim upon your attention at this time.

"HELP-MEET." If the full, rich meaning of this term should be practically illustrated in your matrimonial life, there would be such a bearing of each other's burdens as hope only can depict. You would be *assistants* to each other in the highest import of the word. "Help-meet!" In joy and sorrow delighting to share the allotment with each other! In toils and cares cölaborers together, working with one mind and heart for the same end! At all times anticipating mutual wants, and cheerfully rendering mutual aid! Shoulder to shoulder, heart with heart, hand in hand, thus pursuing the devious path of life!

Ponder it, bridegroom! there is deep meaning in this term that drops so often from "thoughtless tongues." Your chosen wife is an *assistant*, not a doll, or mere household servant and drudge. Your *assistant* in all the "affairs" of home and business. Thus it is with your husband, bride! You have somewhat to do, and he was given you to aid, — not to toil and accumulate wealth that you may lounge on splendid tapestry.

"HELP-MEET!" A sympathizer, counsellor, monitor, co-worker, armor-bearer, assistant.

"ONE!" "They twain shall be one flesh." In all their hopes and interests to be identified with each other, — duality in unity! Two in the material, yet one in the unseen and spiritual! This is the great mystery of married life, — the doctrine of duality in unity, two in one. It is also the great central *truth* of matrimony, around which all others revolve, and without which they are thrown into terrible disorder, and avail nothing. In this connection there is peculiar force in this little word, "ONE." Here it possesses a power of combining, uniting, and almost transfusing, such as it has in no other relation.

When we consider what trifling occurrences have often alienated husband and wife, it appears to be a more difficult and serious matter to be "one." Alas, for the deception of the human heart, and the frailty of human nature! At this very point these two facts are developed in the most humbling manner.

"ONE!" It is the opposite of all unkindness and jealousy, and the absence of even unloving thoughts and emotions. It is a blending of interests and purposes in the great errand of life. It is two currents of affection running into each other,—two hearts "like kindred drops mingling into one."

"One!" No union can be more complete than this. It is impossible for even imagination to conceive of a relation more intimate. And when we reflect that this oneness of spirit once disturbed can never again be perfectly adjusted, it becomes a matter of transcendant interest.

> "If the love of the heart is blighted, it buddeth not again ;
> If that pleasant song is forgotten, it is to be learnt no more."

Often ask yourselves, Are we one? As you go forth from the hymeneal altar you may feel and know that you are one. But, as weeks and months pass away, and cares and perplexities multiply, let the inquiry frequently be made, Are we one? Strive to realize the delightful and yet serious meaning that is wrapped up in this little word. Ever may the following lines be illustrated in your experience:

> "Then come the wild weather,—come sleet or come snow,—
> We will stand by each other, however it blow ;
> Oppression, and sickness, and sorrow and pain,
> Shall be to our true love as links to the chain." *

From this time you will go on learning each other's characters. As yet you are comparative strangers to each other's weaknesses. During the period of courtship there is little opportunity to learn what a person's real

* Longfellow.

virtues or frailties are. The parties usually appear in their best trim as to manners and acquirements. Another has said, "They put on false characters. They assume airs not their own. They shine in borrowed plumes. They practise every species of deception for the concealment of their real characters. They study to appear better than they are. They seek, by the adornments of dress and gems, by the blandishments of art and manner, by the allurement of smiles and honeyed words, by the fascination of pleasure and scenes of excitement, to add unreal, unpossessed charms to their persons and characters. They appear in each other's society to be the embodiment of goodness and sweetness, the personification of lofty principle and holy love, when, in fact, they are full of human weaknesses and frailties."

There is too much truth in the above remarks. And, hence, it is generally the fact that both bride and bridegroom are imperfectly acquainted with each other. At any rate, they are not familiar with one another's *frailties*. These have been so hidden by airs and blandishments as not to be discovered. Not until the aim and art to please are forgotten amid the stern realities of wedded life do they begin to develop themselves. In circumstances of perplexity and trial there is a fine opportunity for their disclosure. In the domestic circle, when familiarity has reached its maximum, there is little or no restraint, and the true character appears. It is not till then that the wedded parties usually know each other beyond a doubt.

Thus may it be with yourselves; and you do well to be prepared for the revelations promised. Come the disclosures will, sooner or later, and it is the part of wisdom to make the best of them. It will be too late then to remedy the evil in another way than bearing with it. The exercise of some of the graces before discussed will then be required as the only remedial policy.

Realize that you will have need, if death does not separate you for many years, of all the counsels contained in this humble volume. As you learn more and more of each other, you will appreciate, with greater accuracy, the mutual duties of the conjugal relation before discussed.

If you endeavor to please each other with as much study and care as you did during your courtship, there is little fear that your union will be unhappy. It is often true, however, that when the parties enter the marriage state they conclude it is no longer necessary to make this effort. The bird is caught, and, bait or no bait, there is no escape. There is a fatal mistake here. There is greater need of this effort to please after than before marriage. More is depending upon it. Yea, the happiness of the entire wedded life is determined by it. If the husband is more studious to please any and everybody else than his own wife, and she, also, is inclined to the same error, farewell to all the joy and harmony of their earthly home. But if the reverse is true, the angel of peace will descend upon their habitation, and the buds and blossoms of hope will spring up and smile in their pathway.

Be wise, then, BRIDAL PAIR, and at the altar, where your connubial bands are tied, ponder the duties of this life-long relation! You cannot give them undue prominence. You cannot unduly magnify your mutual responsibilities. Remember what you have pledged yourselves to do. Forget not your plighted vow. Walk together as "one," till the hand of the great destroyer severs the tie of life. Let memory, affection, hope, and confidence, all be busy to hallow the alliance, and cause you and yours to look back, from future years, with pleasure upon your nuptial day. Live ye as one together in all that appertains to love and duty, and your early friendship will grow and mingle with advancing years, as two trees, planted near each other, interlock their spreading branches and blend their foliage with the flight of years.

Husband! Endearing name, this, which you have now taken to yourself, and one that will sit gracefully upon you, or not, according to your fidelity. It is easy to be unfaithful in this new relation. You have only to be unwatchful, and neglect to nurture the tender plant of love, — to follow the promptings of passion and blind impulse, — and the work is done. But I warn you against any approach to unfaithfulness. Crush not the heart of your devoted wife by an unloving spirit and cruel words. She is more sensitive than thyself. A deeper current of feeling rushes through her soul. The blow, that would scarcely make thee feel, will tear and lacerate her heart. Her love, too, is more constant than thine, and more enduring. Look around you, for a moment, and behold what devotion, on the part of wives, is manifested. See the wife of the domestic tyrant, — a woman taken in her girlhood from the bosom of tenderness and affluence, — now the recipient of all manner of unkindness and abuse; yet meekly demeaning herself under it all, though often trembling before storms of human wrath as a reed shaken by the wind. And still she loves on with an affection that death only can quench. She clings to her tyrant-spouse with the firmness of one in whose fidelity is involved the matter of life or death. Behold the companion of the bloated inebriate amid trials of the most oppressive character. When strong drink has imbruted her husband, and well-nign obliterated the human from his soul, see her still, the same devoted and affectionate partner, soothing him in moments of delirium with honeyed words, and, at all times, laying herself, a living sacrifice, upon the altar of love. Her lookers-on wonder that she will longer live with such a wretch, throwing away her happiness and life upon a worse than worthless man. But they mistake the nature of woman's love. They forget that it is a part of her moral nature to be faithful and true, even when religion seems almost to sanction the opposite. She can never forget her first love and plighted vow; and, hence, the wife of the inebriate clings to him in poverty and distress.

> "Alas! the love of woman! — it is known
> To be a lovely and a fearful thing;
> For all of theirs upon that die is thrown,
> And, if 't is lost, life hath no more to bring
> To them, but mockeries of the past alone."

Ponder this, dear sir, whenever you are disposed to violate the obligations imposed by the marriage contract. In whatever else you may be superior to her, in love and fidelity she is doubtless superior to thee. Neglect her, scorn her, abuse her, and she will love thee still. Prove unfaithful thyself, she will not follow thy example. She is thy companion, — bosom friend; never degrade her below this high position. "A Turk or a Hindoo would feel himself insulted by any inquiry which implied that he regarded his wife as a companion; that he ever consulted her on questions of duty, or stooped to converse with her on important subjects. But the Christian rite of marriage brings together two persons as equals and companions, to enjoy each other's society, and to be mutual counsellors and co-workers. They have, certainly, their separate spheres and duties, and no good can ever come of their exchanging places; but this does not preclude an habitual comparison of views on all subjects of common interest. Many a man has been saved from disastrous speculations by listening to the suggestions of a prudent wife."

While there are marked exceptions to all that has been said of woman, you may rely upon it as true, in the main, of female character.

Never suffer your reputation as husband to be tarnished by the charge of unfaithfulness. Cherish your wife as your "second self." Discharge the various duties to which your attention has been called with promptness, and it will sweeten the cup of connubial joy. She is thy WIFE, — COMPANION. Love her; confide in her; be faithful to the end.

Wife! A new and tender appellation, this, with which you are now greeted. See that you prove yourself a *wife* in very truth; a sharer in the bliss or misery of wedded life; a sympathizer and helper in all the privations, duties, and changes of earthly existence. You have not entered into this relation in order that you may flirt, and gad, and live at ease. Because you have a husband your responsibilities are not diminished; they are rather increased. Your new sphere brings with it new duties, — duties that demand something more than acquaintance with the fine arts, and a taste for fashionable and refined circles. In the language of Hannah More, "Though the arts that embellish life claim admiration, yet, when a man of sense comes to marry, it is a companion he wants, and not an artist. It is not merely a creature who can dress, and paint, and sing; it is a being who can comfort and counsel him; one who can reason, and reflect, and feel, and judge, and act; one who can assist him in his affairs, soothe his sorrows, lighten his cares, purify his joys, and educate his children." This is wise counsel. Treasure it up in your heart, for much depends upon yourself whether your marriage shall prove a happy union. If possible, a wife possesses the greater advantage to render wedded life joyous, and make a happy home. Her husband may not be what she expected to find him, nor such a man as he ought to be; still she can do much to lighten the vexations and trials that arise from his delinquencies, if, indeed, she may not be the happy instrument in making him a better husband.

Act the part of a faithful, noble, trusting, devoted woman. Endeavor to be contented with your allotment. Let no one excel yourself in fidelity. So live as wife that it may be said of you in truth, "She openeth her mouth with wisdom; and in her tongue is the law of kindness. She looketh well to the ways of her household, and eateth not the bread of idleness. Her children arise up and call her blessed; her husband also, and he praiseth her. Many daughters have done virtuously, but thou excellest them all."

One thought more. How frail is the tie that unites you, husband and wife, in the bands of wedlock! Present health and hopes may promise a long and blissful union, but an arrow from the quiver of death may dissipate in a moment your sweetest joys.

"Leaves have their times to fall,
And flowers to wither at the north-wind's breath,
And stars to set, — but all,
Thou hast all seasons for thine own, O death!" *

To-day you may enjoy the fairest promise of life and happiness; to-morrow one of you may weep and agonize over the lifeless remains of the other. So uncertain are earthly ties! So relentless is the great destroyer!

I remember one whom I married, — a bride in her joyous youth and beauty; — the bloom of health was upon her cheek, and the strength of hope was in her heart. A bride never stood at the altar of marriage with brighter prospects of lengthened life and unmingled bliss. Ten swift months passed away, and the fond husband stood over her lifeless form, his disappointed heart almost bursting with grief at the sudden change. She was dead. Quickly as the tempest cuts down a rose of summer, death

* Mrs. Hemans.

removed his victim. Mysterious Providence! Strange vicissitude! Surely life is a "vapor that appeareth for a little while and then vanisheth away!"

I remember another, — a young and faithful husband. It is only a single year since I married him to the lady of his choice; but, now, where is he? A few days since I performed the funeral rites at his burial. The blooming wife pines in lonely widowhood, and says that the world is dark. The bright vision that floated before her mind's eye on the eve of her wedding has vanished as a dream, and she sits lonely and sad, because the foot-fall of her spouse, that was once music to her ear, is not heard in her dwelling. In her sorrow she laments the uncertain tenure of earthly bonds, and, as she goes about the streets, I can read, upon her melancholy brow, the great burden of her heart, "Lover and friend hast thou put far from me, and mine acquaintance into darkness."

Learn from the above a useful lesson, and let it stimulate you to the discharge of mutual duties. No regrets can be more painful than those which are experienced by the faithless in those sacred bonds when death dissolves the union. To follow a companion to the grave, while the soul is oppressed with the consciousness of neglecting or wronging him or her, this must be a more bitter experience than the bereavement itself. When we linger by the coffin or tomb of some beloved friend, memory is busy in retracing the past, and recalling every word, and act, and emotion, inconsistent with the relation that has subsisted between us. If possible, we would blot forever from the past every record of injury and wrong which we have inflicted, that, with hands washed in innocency, we may weep over the stricken loved one. Doubly true is this of unfaithfulness in the conjugal relation.

BE TRUE TO EACH OTHER, — LOVE MUCH, — LIVE JOYFULLY TOGETHER, — BE FAITHFUL UNTO DEATH.

"To meet, to part, to smile,
To shed the frequent tear;
The hope to win, the joy to lose, —
This is our history here;
To find the rose, whose bloom
By no dark blight is riven,
To meet, and never more to part,
Is not of earth, but heaven."

MRS. SIGOURNEY.

POETRY.

I.

THE SAINTED BRIDE.

Loud rang the welkin-dome at morn,
And swift as lightning-lance
The royal welcome, welcome flew
O'er hill and dale of France.
Around the bridal altar pressed
A nation's sparkling pride ;
The changeful crimson came and went
As shadows o'er the bride ;
The king he held, as if a pearl,
The marble hand of the royal girl.

Strange contrast in the wedded pair!
The bride, in summer-bower,
Bloomed into youth, as suns unfold
The petals of a flower;
The bridegroom, from the throne of Kent,
Of proud old Saxon form,
Reared, like the Druid's mistletoe,
'Neath clouds and sweeping storm;
Won by the magic power of love,
The eagle caught the gentle dove.

So stood the Saxon Ethelbert;
His costume marked his life;
Himself a pagan worshipper—
A *saint* his angel-wife.
Strange two such adverse hearts should meet
The wedded race to run!
Strange two opposing streams of life
Should mingle into one!
Had Bertha hope that she could bring
To cross of Christ the pagan king?

On roll the chariot-wheels of time
    Beneath the royal smile !
No queen drank deeper draughts of bliss
    On Britain's sunny isle.
Her orisons went up to God,
    At morn and eventide ;
His richest benison came down
    In answer to the bride ;
The Spirit left the throne to bring
Salvation to the Saxon king.

II.

THE ADIEU.

My pulse is running low, love,
    The world is fading fast;
My eyes are growing dim, love,
    And life will soon be past.

The king is at the door, love,
    I hear his pleasant voice;
I 'll meet him with a smile, love,
    It is his gracious choice.

Our voyage has been long, love,
    O'er the stormy sea of life;
You 've been a faithful spouse, love,
    And I a happy wife.

Together we have bowed, love,
In sorrow's fiercest gale;
My soul has found thee true, love,
From the time of setting sail.

Now the Master calleth me, love,
You a little longer stay,
To toss a season yet, love,
On the dark and stormy way.

I 'll land ahead of thee, love,
On the bright and sunny shore;
But cheer thy doting heart, love,
Thy voyage soon is o'er.

Why fall the streaming tears, love?
Thou art ever kind and true;
And tell me, ere I go, love,
Have I not been to you?

Our parting will be short, love,
How swift the moments fly!
Our joy will be higher, love,
In mansions in the sky.

I see the haven bright, love,
 And angel-spirits wait,
To give me cordial welcome, love,
 At the fair and pearly gate.

O, ask me not to stay, love,
 On this rough and rolling main !
I see the land of glory, love,
 And there we 'll meet again.

My heart still clings to thee, love,
 In plighted faith, and true ;
We 'll meet on Canaan's shore, love,
 Till then, till then,—adieu !

III.

TWO HEARTS ONE.

As rivers from the hills unite,
 And to the ocean run;
So life presents the cheerful sight,
 Two loving hearts in ONE.

Two toiling hands, — two speaking eyes, —
 Two treasures to be won;
Two souls to fashion for the skies, —
 And yet the two hearts ONE.

One — in the common aims of life;
 One — in the glowing hope to live;
One — in the tug of mortal strife;
 One — in all that earth can give.

One — for the hour of hope at hand;
One — for the trial-scene;
One — for every clime and land;
One — for the grave, I ween.

One — in the bonds of love sincere,
That joy nor woe can sever;
One — in the plighted vow, so dear
That time can blot it — never.

Strange, mystic power! love's power to bless
The wedded moments while they run;
And, as the life-sands number less,
Still keep the two hearts ONE.

IV.

THE BACHELOR'S SOLILOQUY.

"'T IS said I 'm neither loving nor wise
To travel alone the journey of life;
I ne'er shall know the sweetest of ties,
If I take not a woman to wife:—
They do not see the bliss of my heart;
Within it there dwells not a sigh;
Of pleasure I take a generous part;
A happy old bachelor, I!

"I can go and return as I please,
And be out 'fair weather or foul,'
Live, in summer and winter, at ease,
Without meeting a womanly scowl;—

I am tied to no quarter of earth ;
  My comforts are neither dying nor dead ;
I have no cares to stifle my mirth,
  And no children crying for bread.

"When I 've a surplus dollar in hand,
  I merrily use the treasure alone,
Nor have to cut with a family-band
  Of a dozen or more of my own :
Alas ! for the man with a hungering brood,
  With opening mouths, hot weather and cold ;
He needs to increase his portion of food,
  Like the loaves and fishes of old.

"I cozily sleep in my dormitory,
  Though it scarcely measures eight by ten,
And lies, 't is true, in the second story ;
  So even sleep some Congress men ; —
But cheerily look ! no cradle 's there ;
  From the trundling-bed a kind release !
And a richer treat, — no baby fair
  With tiniest cry disturbs the peace.

"I pity the men who toil and sweat,
    In slavery lead such hapless lives,
To garnish a home, and keep in debt
    And doing it all to please their wives.
How servile are *they!* How free am *I!*
    I bless my stars with exulting breast,
I never have known a nuptial sigh,
    Nor yielded part of my cozy nest.

"'T is sure a lottery after all,
    This choosing a partner, young and gay;
Some husband a prize exceeding small,
    And some, they carry a *blank* away; —
I'll never be burned for folly here,
    Nor thorned within this nuptial thicket;
When the girls are all they *seem* to be,
    I'll try, perhaps, a single ticket.

"There's Blaney, the clerk, so neat and trim,
    No 'mother's son' is truer than he;
But his wife 's a 'thorn in the flesh' to him,
    Yea — Xantippe the Second, is she.

He 's driven about from 'pillar to post,'
And really has no comfort of life;
Frolic and fun were ever his boast,
Till he married a troublesome wife.

"And Jerold, the rich, — so people say, —
With his princely mansion, coach and four,
Scarce ever enjoyed a genial day
Behind his front mahogany door.
Whether true or not, — 't is certain that strife
Survived his death and family cares:
For he left behind a scolding wife,
And a parcel of quarrelling heirs.

"E'en Paley, the parson, — a good man too, —
I love to hear his sonorous voice, —
Has cursed the day, if report be true,
That ever he made so bad a choice.
'T is said, — I would not utter it loud,
His fame is pure as the dew of Hermon, —
One day his wife, both fiery and proud,
Burned up in wrath a new-made sermon.

"No! no! I will not, cannot wed,
When wedlock brings such pains and sighing;
If friends could bear it, living and dead,
One half the husbands would be crying.
No! no! I'm chary of 'number one;'
My purse and joy I'm bent on keeping,
When into the snare you see me run,
You'll catch, forsooth, 'a weasel sleeping.'"

So saying, he curled his haughty lip
With a look quite sophomoric,
And, then, the following words let slip,
With an air of the bacheloric:—
"No! no! for me no woman shall try
The cup of wedded joy to mingle;
Let others do as they may,—but I
Will take my blessedness single."

Cool Reason saw with a piercing eye,
Indignant bit his quivering lip,
And, letting the lash of invective fly,
Upon the bachelor laid his whip:—

"Dare thou, O man! for pleasure and pelf,
So niggardly scorn the marriage vow?
'T would shame good mother Eve herself,
If half of her sons were small as thou.

"Go to, and flatter your loveless soul;
Crawl into your shell, as turtle quite;
Think of the fox, who formerly stole
Into the vineyard of clusters bright;
If ever allured by the ripening fruit,
All clustering o'er the nuptial bower,
Perhaps some blasted hope 't will suit
To murmur the cry, '*the grapes are sour!*'"

V.

LIFE'S VOYAGE.

Our life is a voyage with hardships to brave,
From its dawn in the cradle to its end in the grave;
Each breath of our being is driving us on,
As swift on the billows as others have gone;
The port we are making, whether stormy or fair,
For swift we are sailing, and soon shall be there.

Now fortune is coming her pledges to bring,
As sweetly and gayly as queen of the spring;
Now sorrows invade as a storm in the sky,
And hope in the bud is stricken to die;
So changeful the weather of life as we sail, —
Now stilled by the calm, — then tossed by the gale.

To-day we discover a bark sailing fair,
And the merry crew singing, "We soon shall be there;"
To-morrow the drama puts on a new dress;
There floats from the mast the flag of distress,
With the current of life, all flowing and warm,
The brothers, ill-fated, go down in the storm.

Then let us look up to our God, and implore
That his Spirit may waft us safe to the shore;
That breezes propitious his mercy may send,
As when we first cleared, till the passage shall end;
We 're bound for a haven of bliss or despair,
On, on we are sailing, — and soon shall be there.

VI.

LOVE.

Love kindles in the speaking eye,
As light illumes the morning sky;
Now beaming forth in sunny smile,
As if a fairy's pleasant wile;
Then flashing through a silent tear,
As diamond in a fountain clear.

It rules within the heart's domain,
Though every hope of fortune wane;
Sways thought and feeling, hope and will,
From torrent-rush to gentle rill;
Exalts to pleasures, pure and bright,
Nor glooms the heart in sorrow's night.

It nestles in the cradle there,
To bless the child with flaxen hair;
To middle life imparts a ray
Of light to gild each passing day;
Nor leaves to bitter sighs and tears
The old man's heart of eighty years.

It fairest shines in bridal bower,
When merry flies the fleeting hour,
And chosen partners, groom and bride,
As two trees planted side by side,
Unite to breast the gales that sweep
O'er life-paths where the single weep.

Woe quenches not the kindled flame;
Time hastens on, — 't is still the same;
Change dashes hopes and castles fair,
And still the flame is burning there;
Nor dies, — though fanned by care nor art,
Till death seals up the throbbing heart.

VII.

HOPE.

Hope guides our little bark so frail;
On refluent tide she trims the sail;
And points us to her luring star,
More bright than lustrous diamonds are.

Hope cheers when darkness veils the hour;
When storms of sorrow rudely lower,
Her bow of promise arches high
The veiling cloud upon the sky.

Hope never yields her throne of power,
In youth or age, in field or bower;
But doth her golden sceptre wave,
On from the cradle to the grave.

In palace-hall, and lowly cot,
In foreign clime, and natal spot,
In bridal home, and parting scene,
Hope lures to islet ever green.

Hope lives in death; prepared to die,
She bears us to the peaceful sky,
To strike our harps in mansions fair,
And take our crowns of glory there.

VIII.

BROKEN TIES.

Is there a clime where kindred dear
Can wipe their weeping eyes?
A land where drops no farewell tear
O'er parting life, and loved one's bier,
All free from broken ties?

Earth cannot boast a clime so fair,
To lure the grieving soul;
Let love the sweetest bower prepare, —
Sorrow and death will enter there,
And break the "golden bowl."

The bird that doth the sweetest lay
From tree or forest pour;

The fairest flower that blooms in May,
And dearest friends, will pass away,
And be to us no more.

Love twines her tendrils, — winning art! —
With soft and flexile rings,
Around the earthly idol's heart; —
Death from his quiver hurls a dart,
And snaps the slender things.

The tearful group, the tolling bell,
The friend that stricken lies,
The sighs from bleeding hearts that swell,
The coffin, bier and grave, — all tell
A tale of broken ties.

E'en hope like thine, fond, bridal pair!
That cheers the loving heart,
Will vanish as a thing of air,
When death's resistless fingers tear
The "silver cords" apart.

But one blest land is free from woe;
"Land ever bright and fair!"
Rivers of pleasure through it flow,
And fragrant breezes o'er it blow,—
No ties are broken there.

Sweet solace on this changeful shore,
When earthly bonds are riven;—
There is a land where tears are o'er,
And sighs and partings are no more;—
No broken ties in heaven.

www.ingramcontent.com/pod-product-compliance
Lightning Source LLC
LaVergne TN
LVHW021429110826
845150LV00007B/2148

* 9 7 8 1 4 2 5 5 0 7 5 3 4 *